W9-CKM-556

SUPER SIMPLE
EARTH INVESTIGATIONS

SUPER SIMPLE
FOSSIL
PROJECTS

Science Activities for
Future Paleontologists

JESSIE ALKIRE

CONSULTING EDITOR, DIANE CRAIG, M.A./READING SPECIALIST

Super Sandcastle

An Imprint of Abdo Publishing
abdopublishing.com

abdopublishing.com

Published by Abdo Publishing, a division of ABDO, PO Box 398166, Minneapolis, Minnesota 55439. Copyright © 2018 by Abdo Consulting Group, Inc. International copyrights reserved in all countries. No part of this book may be reproduced in any form without written permission from the publisher. Super SandCastle™ is a trademark and logo of Abdo Publishing.

Printed in the United States of America, North Mankato, Minnesota
102017
012018

THIS BOOK CONTAINS RECYCLED MATERIALS

Design: Kelly Doudna, Mighty Media, Inc.
Production: Mighty Media, Inc.
Editor: Liz Salzmann
Cover Photographs: Mighty Media, Inc.; Shutterstock
Interior Photographs: iStockphoto; Mighty Media, Inc.; Shutterstock; Wikimedia Commons

The following manufacturers/names appearing in this book are trademarks: Argo®, Elmer's®, Equaline®, Gold Medal®, Pyrex®, Reynolds® Cut-Rite®, Strathmore®, 3M™, You Paint It!™

Publisher's Cataloging-in-Publication Data

Names: Alkire, Jessie, author.
Title: Super simple fossil projects: science activities for future paleontologists / by Jessie Alkire.
Other titles: Science activities for future paleontologists
Description: Minneapolis, Minnesota : Abdo Publishing, 2018. | Series: Super simple earth investigations
Identifiers: LCCN 2017946516 | ISBN 9781532112379 (lib.bdg.) | ISBN 9781614799795 (ebook)
Subjects: LCSH: Paleontology--Juvenile literature. | Fossils--Juvenile literature. | Science--Experiments--Juvenile literature.
Classification: DDC 507.8--dc23
LC record available at https://lccn.loc.gov/2017946516

Super SandCastle™ books are created by a team of professional educators, reading specialists, and content developers around five essential components—phonemic awareness, phonics, vocabulary, text comprehension, and fluency—to assist young readers as they develop reading skills and strategies and increase their general knowledge. All books are written, reviewed, and leveled for guided reading and early reading intervention programs for use in shared, guided, and independent reading and writing activities to support a balanced approach to literacy instruction.

TO ADULT HELPERS

The projects in this title are fun and simple. There are just a few things to remember. Kids may be using messy materials such as glue or paint. Make sure they protect their clothes and work surfaces. Review the projects before starting, and be ready to assist when necessary.

CONTENTS

WHAT IS A FOSSIL?

A fossil is the remains or traces of a living thing. This can be a plant, insect, or animal. The remains are preserved in rock. Fossils take thousands of years to form. Some take millions!

PETRIFIED FOSSIL

Fossils are important. They tell scientists about what life was like long ago. Scientists can learn how plants and animals have changed.

Some fossils form through petrification. This is when **minerals** enter the remains. Conditions must be just right for petrification to occur.

The remains need to be buried quickly. Then **minerals** fill spaces in the remains. The minerals harden the remains into a fossil.

Fossils can also be found in amber. And some fossils are molds. These are **impressions** from the preserved remains.

MOLD FOSSIL

TYPES OF FOSSILS

There are two main types of fossils.
They are body fossils and trace fossils.

BODY FOSSILS

Body fossils are the remains or imprints of an animal or plant. Bones are body fossils. So are teeth, shells, leaves, and branches. Body fossils are the most common type of fossil.

TRACE FOSSILS

Trace fossils show activity from long ago. Footprints and tracks are trace fossils. So is an ancient animal's **burrow**. Trace fossils give clues about an animal's behavior. They can tell how an animal moved, ate, or slept.

HOW SCIENTISTS STUDY FOSSILS

Some scientists study fossils. They are called paleontologists.

Many fossils are buried underground. Fossils are easily broken. Paleontologists must remove them carefully.

Scientists study the fossils in labs. They do tests to learn how old the fossils are. They try to find out what plant or animal the fossil came from.

This **research** helps scientists learn about Earth long ago. They see how plants and animals have changed over time.

PALEONTOLOGISTS USE BRUSHES TO GENTLY UNCOVER FOSSILS.

MARY ANNING

Mary Anning was an English paleontologist in the 1800s. She lived in England. She started fossil hunting with her family when she was a child. The family sold the fossils to earn money. During her life, Anning made many important discoveries. One of these was the first complete Plesiosaurus skeleton. She found it in 1824.

ANNING IS ALSO KNOWN FOR FINDING THE FIRST ICHTHYOSAUR FOSSIL.

MATERIALS

Here are some of the materials that you will need for the projects in this book.

BORAX DETERGENT BOOSTER

CLAY

CLEAR GLUE

COFFEE GROUNDS

CORNSTARCH

EPSOM SALT

FLOUR

FOOD COLORING

MASKING TAPE

MEASURING CUPS

MEASURING SPOONS

NEWSPAPER

PAINTBRUSH

PAPER TOWEL

PLASTER OF PARIS

SCREWDRIVER

SHALLOW CONTAINER

SMOOTH-SIDED JAR OR GLASS

SPONGES

TOOTHPICK

VEGETABLE OIL

WATERCOLOR PAINTS

WATERCOLOR PAPER

WAX PAPER

TIPS AND TECHNIQUES

Paleontologists use some simple tools to dig up fossils. These include small shovels, **chisels**, screwdrivers, and brushes. To break a rock, hold a screwdriver against it. Then hit the top of the handle with a hammer. Hit it gently at first, then harder if necessary.

PLASTER FOSSILS

MATERIALS: clay, wax paper, smooth-sided jar or glass, vegetable oil, paper towel, small fossil objects (toys, leaves, shells, rubber stamps), water, measuring cups, bowl, plaster of Paris, spoon, cardboard, toothpick

Some plants or animals leave an **impression** in rock. This is a mold. The mold can be filled by **minerals**. This creates a cast.

1 **Knead** a ball of clay until it softens.

2 Set the clay on a sheet of wax paper. Roll the jar on the clay to flatten it. Make it big enough for one or more fossil objects to fit on it.

3 Put a little vegetable oil on a paper towel. Rub the oil on your fossil objects. This will keep them from sticking to the clay.

Continued on the next page.

4 Press an object slowly but firmly into the clay.

5 Remove the object and observe the **impression** your object made. This will be the mold for the plaster!

6 Repeat steps 4 and 5 with other fossil objects.

7 Put 1 cup of water in a mixing bowl.

8 Slowly add 2 cups of plaster of Paris powder. Sprinkle it over the water a little at a time. Mix well after each addition. It should become as thick as pancake batter.

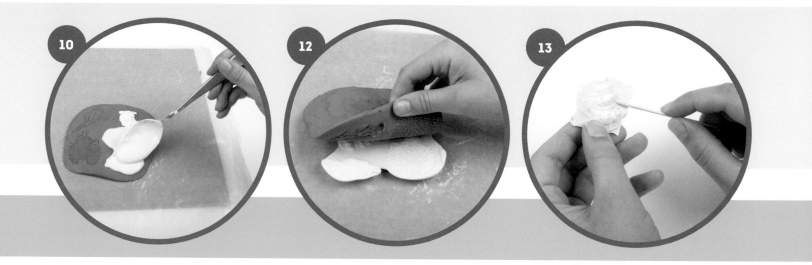

⑨ Move the wax paper and clay mold onto a piece of cardboard.

⑩ Fill the **impressions** in the clay with the plaster mixture. Smooth the plaster with a spoon to make a flat surface.

⑪ Wait for the plaster to harden. This takes about 30 minutes.

⑫ Peel the clay mold from your plaster casts. The impression of each object should be recreated in the plaster!

⑬ Use a toothpick to gently remove any extra pieces of clay from the casts.

DINOSAUR BONE ART

MATERIALS: internet-connected computer or books about dinosaurs, pencil, dinosaur stencil (optional), watercolor paper, marker, masking tape, scissors, watercolor paints, paintbrush, cup, water

Many fossils are dinosaur bones. Some are full dinosaur skeletons! Dinosaur skeletons are often displayed in museums. Paleontologists still find new dinosaur bones today.

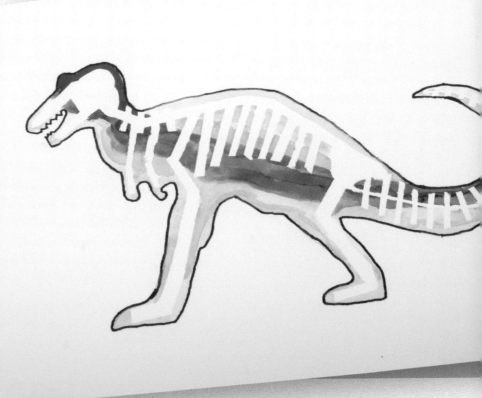

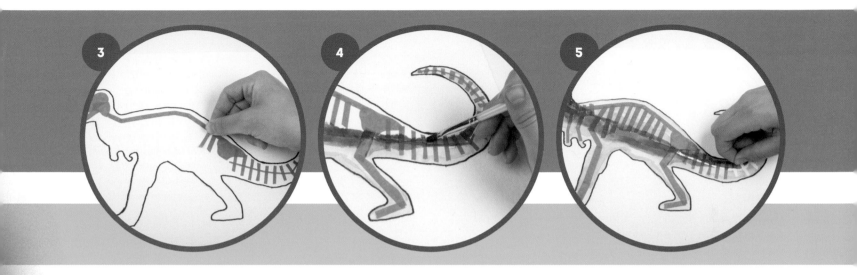

① Study images of dinosaur bones and skeletons to get an idea of what they look like.

② Use a pencil to draw or trace the outline of a dinosaur on watercolor paper. Go over the pencil lines with marker.

③ Place small pieces of masking tape in the dinosaur outline where the bones should be.

④ Paint the dinosaur with watercolors. Paint over the tape. Let the paint dry.

⑤ Remove the tape. The white areas where the tape was look like dinosaur bones!

FOSSIL EXCAVATION

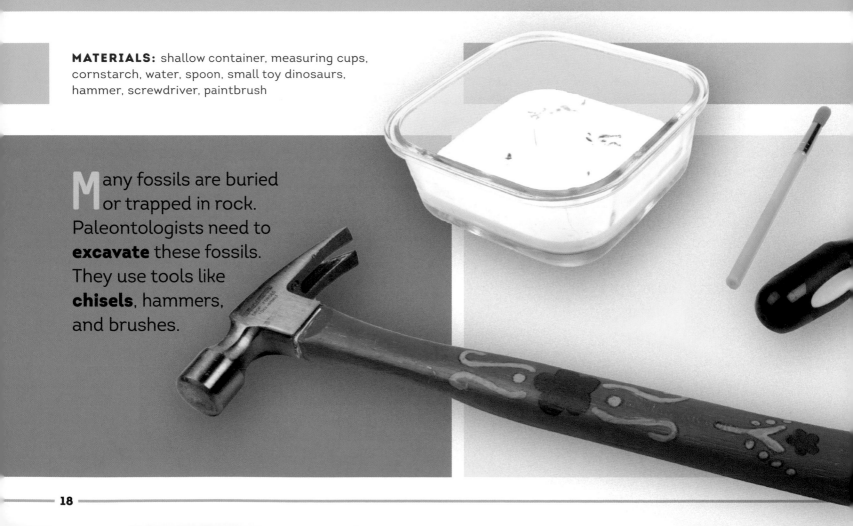

MATERIALS: shallow container, measuring cups, cornstarch, water, spoon, small toy dinosaurs, hammer, screwdriver, paintbrush

Many fossils are buried or trapped in rock. Paleontologists need to **excavate** these fossils. They use tools like **chisels**, hammers, and brushes.

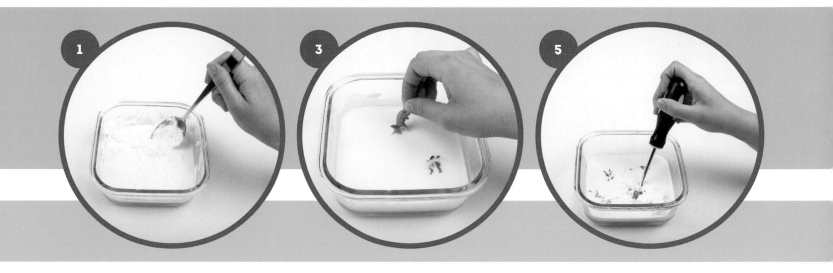

1 Mix two parts cornstarch to one part water in the container. The mixture should be deep enough to cover the toy dinosaurs.

2 The cornstarch should be completely wet, but the mixture shouldn't be runny. If necessary, adjust by adding more cornstarch or water.

3 Push the toy dinosaurs into the mixture.

4 Set the container where it will get sunlight during the day. Leave it there to dry for one to two days.

5 Use the hammer, screwdriver, paintbrush, or other tools to **excavate** your fossils. Refer to the Tips and Techniques on page 11. Be careful not to break the fossils!

6 Use a paintbrush to dust the dinosaurs off.

AMBER FOSSIL SLIME

MATERIALS: measuring cup, water, small bowl, measuring spoon, Borax Detergent Booster, mixing spoon, large bowl, 5-ounce (142 g) bottle of clear glue, red & yellow food coloring, plastic toy insects

Not all fossils are in rock. Some fossils are trapped in amber. Amber is a **substance** made of hardened resin.

1 Put 1 cup of water into a small bowl.

2 Add 2 teaspoons of Borax. Mix well. Set the bowl aside.

3 Put ½ cup of water in a large bowl.

4 Slowly add the entire bottle of clear glue. Mix well.

5 Add one drop of red food coloring and two drops of yellow food coloring to the glue mixture. Mix well.

Continued on the next page.

6 Pour the Borax mixture into the glue mixture.

7 Stir the ingredients well. Thick **slime** should start to form quickly.

8 Remove the slime from the bowl and pour out any extra water. Place the slime back in the bowl.

9 Add the toy insects to the slime. Push them completely into the slime.

10 Set the slime aside. In about a day it will become solid but squishy, kind of like gelatin.

11 Take the slime out of the bowl. Observe the insects. They're trapped in the slime just like insects in amber fossils!

12 Store your amber fossil slime in a sealed container. You can also leave the slime out to harden further like real amber!

DIGGING DEEPER

Amber is a hard, orange-yellow **substance** often found near the shores of lakes and oceans. Amber often has insect fossils inside it. Amber forms from a sticky liquid called resin which is produced by trees. Insects get trapped in the resin. When the trees die and break apart, the resin falls off. Water from rain and rivers carries the resin to lakes and oceans. The resin gets buried in layers of rock under the water. The resin slowly hardens into amber. The process takes millions of years!

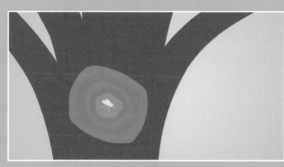

INSECT TRAPPED IN RESIN

TREE DIES AND RESIN FALLS OFF

RIVER CARRIES RESIN TO BODY OF WATER

RESIN TURNS INTO AMBER

SPONGE FOSSIL PERMINERALIZATION

MATERIALS: sponges, marker, scissors, large bowl, measuring cup, hot tap water, Epsom salt, spoon, pitcher, small bowls

One fossilization process is permineralization. This is when a plant's or an animal's remains get full of water. **Minerals** in the water form hard crystals in the open spaces in the remains.

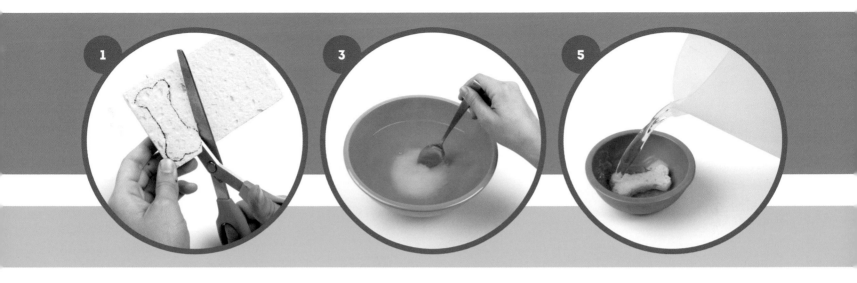

1 Draw bone shapes on sponges. Cut them out. These will be your fossils.

2 Put about 6 cups of hot water in a bowl.

3 Add a large spoonful of Epsom salt to the water. Stir until the salt **dissolves**. Keep stirring in spoonfuls of Epsom salt until no more will dissolve.

4 Pour the salt water into a pitcher.

5 Put each bone fossil into its own small bowl. Pour salt water over each bone until the bone is covered with water.

6 Wait for the sponges to **absorb** the water. Pour out any extra water from the bowls.

7 Leave the sponges to dry. This can take a few days. Once dry, the sponge fossils should be hard as rocks. This is permineralization at work!

DINOSAUR EGGS

MATERIALS: large bowl, measuring cups, flour, coffee grounds, sand, salt, spoon, water, small toy dinosaurs, plastic plate, newspaper, hammer, screwdriver, paintbrush

Some dinosaur eggs never hatched. Instead, they became fossils. But these fossils are rare. Rocks are often mistaken for dinosaur egg fossils. Paleontologists know how to recognize a dinosaur egg. One thing they look for is lines on the surface. The lines are from cracks in the egg's shell.

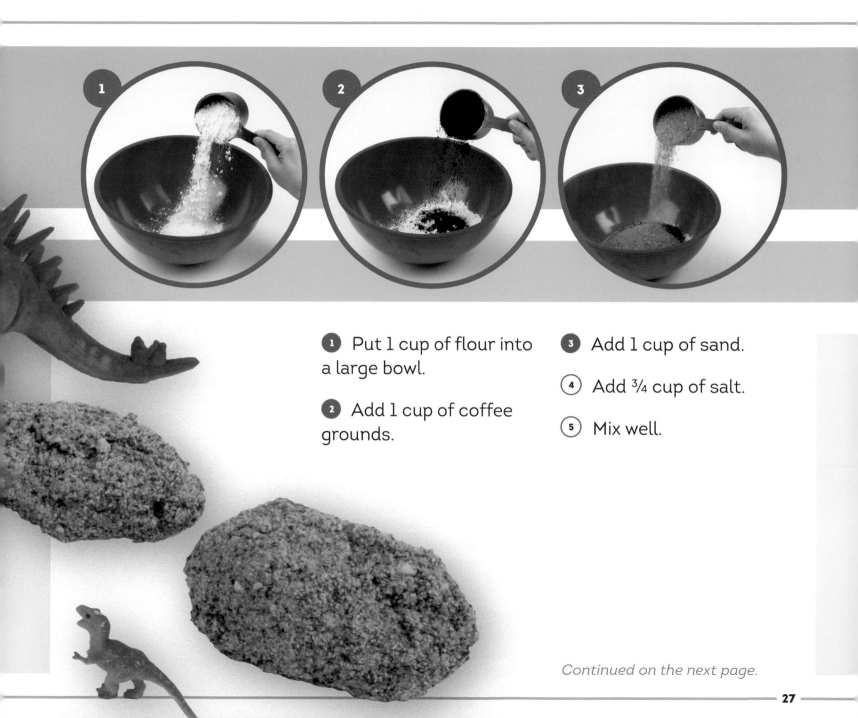

1 Put 1 cup of flour into a large bowl.

2 Add 1 cup of coffee grounds.

3 Add 1 cup of sand.

4 Add ¾ cup of salt.

5 Mix well.

Continued on the next page.

6 Mix in just enough water so that you can form the mixture into a ball that stays together.

7 Take a handful of the mixture and place a toy dinosaur on top.

8 Add more of the mixture on top of the dinosaur. Press the mixture around the dinosaur.

9 Add more of the mixture until it forms a ball around the dinosaur. Roll the ball in your hands until it forms an egg shape.

10 Repeat steps 7 through 9 with the other toy dinosaurs.

11 Place the eggs on a plate. Let them dry for a few days. Turn the eggs each day so they dry evenly.

12 Once dry, place the eggs on newspaper. Use paleontologist tools to break the dinosaur eggs open! Refer to the Tips and Techniques on page 11.

13 Use a paintbrush to dust the dinosaurs off.

Dinosaur egg fossils are often found in nests. Dinosaur eggs come in many shapes and sizes. It is rare to find preserved remains inside the egg. Paleontologists study the eggs. They learn about dinosaurs' reproduction and parenting behaviors. They try to find out what kind of dinosaur the egg came from.

NEST OF FOSSILIZED DINOSAUR EGGS

CONCLUSION

Fossils are the remains of ancient plants and animals. Paleontologists study fossils to learn what Earth was like long ago. They find out how animals and plants have changed over time. This can help us prepare for changes to Earth in the **future**.

QUIZ

1. What fills spaces in remains during petrification?

2. Footprints are body fossils.
   TRUE OR FALSE?

3. In which country did Mary Anning live?

LEARN MORE ABOUT IT!

You can find out more about fossils at the library. Or you can ask an adult to help you **research** fossils **online**!

GLOSSARY

absorb – to to soak up or take in.

burrow – a hole or tunnel in the ground that is used for shelter.

chisel – a tool with a flat, sharp end.

dissolve – to become part of a liquid.

excavate – to uncover something by digging away and removing the dirt that covers it.

future – time that hasn't happened yet.

impression – a mark or an effect made by something.

knead – to press and squeeze with your hands.

mineral – a chemical element or compound that occurs naturally in the ground.

online – connected to the Internet.

research – 1. the act of finding out more about something. 2. to find out more about something.

slime – a slippery, soft substance.

substance – anything that takes up space, such as a solid object or a liquid.